VAMPIRE RESSURRECTION:

THE DAWN OF LOVE AND HORROR

BY

HENRY WEST

TABLE OF CONTENTS

CHAPTER ONE
Lost in the Abyss

I opened my eyes to grab a bird that was trying to feed on my skin.

Where the hell am I ?

I looked down and was shocked to find myself lying in a garbage.

Holly Molly!

What in the world am I doing in a garbage? Could it be that I have gone naughts? But I am thinking straight right now, so it definitely means that I am still in my right senses.

I quickly stood up and dusted my clothe. I was in a lost state, more like a lost person; I wish I knew who I am but it's so difficult to remember. I tried to think harder on how I got here but I was hurting my skull by thinking.

How is this possible?

How could my skull hurt when I try to think it is so ridiculous. I looked at myself and realized I was putting on a suit. The suit looked quiet expensive, could it be that I am from a rich home? I smiled at the thoughts of coming from a rich home.

Filled with curiosity, I dipped my hand into my chest pocket to check if I could find any Identity card or any clue on me. But there was none rather I felt a liquid, I hurriedly pulled off my hand and to my shrill, my hand was covered with blood.

 I opened my suit to find a large hole on my chest; it was big enough to cause much pain to me, but I wasn't feeling any pain. I became more confused of what I am .

What in heaven's sake is going on?

Still filled with confusion and fear of the unknown, I got out of the garbage and moved up to a hill near by. I could access the city from here and surprisingly, I recognize the city. I was in Frankfurt!

But the question is, how did I get here and where did I come from? What am I ? A ghost? Or a demon? Why don't I feel pain? And why am I still alive if I have such a hole in my heart? Aren't I supposed to be a human?
Too many questions to ask but no one to answer.

I sighed and moved down the hill into a rainforest vegetation. I

kept on walking with no particular destination in mind. I suddenly heard a noise nearby; I tried to run behind a tree but I was still moving slowly. I couldn't move fast enough.
I became tensed.

"Woo woo woof!" Came the sound of barking dogs, it seems like it sensed me; it must be a hunting dog.

What if the hunter finds me? Will he kill me, seeing that I don't behave like a human? I have to do something about this. I cant get caught by the dog.

As the dog was approaching, something absurd began to occur; I started to perceive an enticing aroma from the dog and suddenly there arouse a strong urge to feed on whatever was emitting such sweet aroma.I felt like eating the beast!
The nearer it got to me, the more the aroma increased.

What the heck? What is happening to me? I tried to cover my nose, probably this would prevent me from sniffing the aroma but I couldn't move my hand. It felt as if I was being controlled by an external force.

I couldn't wait anymore, I lost my reasoning ability, my eyes turned red and all I was bent on doing was having a taste of the dog!

I turned immediately with red eyes to the direction of the aroma. it was a German shepherd but I didn't care! I have to feed on it and it must be now!

And like the speed of a light, I scurried to the direction of the barking dog. I quickly came to a halt few meters to where the dog stood. I sniffed as I perceived another stronger aroma, apart from that of the dog.

"Hey who are you?" A man howled. I looked up to see a man holding unto a chain which was tightly tied to a German shepherd. He had a torch in his hand and the few wrinkles on his face shows that he was an elderly man, probably in his late fifties. Could he be a hunter?

"Hey! I am talking to you young man. Who the fuck are you and what the fuck are you doing here by this hour of the night?" The man asked again and pointed the torch at me. The light caused my eyes to hurt and I quickly covered them with my hand.

Looks like the hunter realized his mistake and put off the torch. I forcefully opened my eyes and once again the urge to feed on both the human and dog arouse again.

I didn't actually know why they produced such aroma; but the urge to eat them was growing so intense.
I rushed towards the man and stretched forth my hand to grab his neck but paused. What am I doing? This is not right. I can't eat my fellow human.

I struggled with whatever was controlling me, I just can't eat a human. The force seemed stronger but I wasn't willing to give in. I had a feeling that once I give in, I would never be able to go back again and I don't want that. I don't want to be a monster.

 I was still lost in my thoughts when I suddenly felt a hand pushed me backwards causing me to fall hard to the ground.

The hunter hurriedly pinned me to the floor.

"I said, who the freaking fuck are you weirdo?" He roared.

Why does he keep asking me this same question that I was asking myself a while ago? I also don't know who I am. But just now, I almost ate a human and a dog. Not just that, I also wanted to eat them raw. So does that make me a..

8

I widened my eyes in shock as the thought of being a vampire or a zombie flashed my mind.

No! I cant be a vampire or zombie, I cant be one; This is so terrible.

CHAPTER TWO
survival

"I said who are you and why are you here by this time? Don't you know that this is a restricted area?"

I had to control the hunger sensation in my stomach although it was almost impossible to do that. I was loosing control of my body and the worst part of the whole scenario is that I couldn't even talk.

"Oh! I see you drank yourself to stupor and you don't know your way back home?" The man suddenly exclaimed and burst out laughing. I was relieved for a while, I thought he was probably going to mistake me for an arm robber, I would prefer he dose that.

"Such a big fool! Now get out of here you scumbag"

I felt bad but at the same time delighted to know that he was going to allow me leave without finding out what I am. Maybe he is the scumbag.

I looked at the man and it was as if I could see through him; his green and rigid red veins where clearly visible in his face and his heart was beating in a good rhythm. "sup freak? What are you looking at Hugh? Get the fuck out of here man'.

He pointed the way out of the forest to me and I followed it carefully while the dog never stopped barking at me.

Maybe it knows what I am. Just stop barking, I shouldn't have spared your miserable life.

With the help of the forest guard or maybe hunter, I arrived in front of a movie cinema. I was battling so strong with my urge to eat the humans I came across.

Please help me God, why do I keep having this weird urge?.

I found a hoodie on the ground, I quickly picked it up and put it on. My suit already has few stains of blood from the hole in my heart, so I had to cover it up to avoid drawing suspicions.

From the back of a large tree where I stood, I watched the humans talk, laugh, walk in and out of the cinema and I wanted to be like that as well, to be able to smile and do things just like everyone out here. I just wanted to be like them. I decided that I was going to adapt. I will do everything possible to kill this beast I am gradually turning into.

Why would I want to eat my fellow humans? Did I just say fellow? Although I am not sure of what I am but I know that its not close to human being; but nevertheless I wouldn't have to eat them if I will like to be left alive.

"woof woo woo woof"

Another dog again? I think everybody in this neighborhood has a dog! I must find my way out of here, before this dogs ends up sniffing out who I am or probably draw suspicions to me.

 But where do I go? And how do I go there?

I was still contemplating when I suddenly felt the pocket of the hoodie vibrate.

Oh shit! There is a cell phone in this dumb hoodie. And it is ringing already.
Why now? Why in a place like this? I hope I don't get caught by people.

 "Over there Sophia! I heard the phone ring at the back of that tree over there!" I heard someone call out.

Damn it! So this hoodie belongs to a lady? No wonder it has a unique aroma. I have to remove it and get out of here soon before they think I stole it from her.

I tried to put my hands into the hoodie and throw away the phone but my hand refused to move. My body felt so stiff! I felt so useless. Why is this happening now? Gosh! I am doomed. I am screwed up.

"Hey mister" I heard a feminine voice say, I looked up to behold one of the most prettiest face I have seen since I became conscious. The lady had a fascinating brown eyes with pointed nose and tiny lips. She was blonde and elegant and her long hair flew freely down her shoulders.

"Sorry that's my hoodie and I think I left my phone inside it!. Can you just help me with it?" She spoke softly.

I couldn't reply. I just kept staring at her as she spoke.

"You could have the hoodie for yourself and also ten euro that is inside it, but I actually need the phone for my job."

I swallowed hard.

" Sir please say something. Sir! Sir! Sir!"

Why does she keeps on calling me Sir? We're almost of the same age or should I say, she looked a little bit younger than me.

I let out a sigh and try to move my hand again but to no avail, it just refused to move.

Oh I am doomed. She should just put her hand in the right pocket and take the phone. My damn hands are so stiff why cant they just move? God please help me I don't want to die like this.

"Sir, please sir. sir I can top up the 10 euro for you. Sir please just mention your prize.. " She cried, causing some people to turn to our direction.

Oh God! She has started attracting the attention of passers by. I wish I could just get out of here. Or should I explain my condition to her? No. She might not understand. What if she freaks out? Exactly she will definitely freak out. Well, I cant even tell her anything since my mouth isn't opening . seems like my body is getting more stiff and I am almost loosing control of fighting back my hunger sensation.

"Hey whats going on there"

I know this voice! Yes! The smell is also familiar; I looked up and saw the forest guard that drove me out of the rainforest. Now he has a reason to kill me! Damn it.

"I said whats going on here and why are you shouting?" He asked again.

Thank goodness! My face was covered with the hoodie . I quickly bowed my head to make my face more hidden.

"Oh! Is that your husband you are talking to? Poor lady! Looks like he has drank himself to stupor and now he cant go with you! This is the reason why I always advise my daughters not to get married to poor men" The security guard let out a brief laughter.
" Well family will always have problems don't you think so?".

I knew it, this man is not just dumb but also insensitive, But will she actually tell him what is happening or just keep staring at the forest guard?

"Sir it's not what you think. He has my cell phone and he is hesitating to give it to me. Please help me sir" she said with a sobbing tone.

Fuck me, she actually did.

"What? A pervert in Frankfurt! I will kill him myself" He exclaimed. "Hey. Show your face you pervert! Now!!!"

I felt my heart miss a beat.

"I said show me your face you pervert" The man yelled and pulled off the cover of the hoodie vehemently and I looked up in great horror.

"Drunk scumbag? I know you! I thought I told you to stay out of this vicinity Hugh?"

I swallowed hard, staring at him blankly and wondering what might be his next actions.

He suddenly let out a scary laughter. "I guess you don't know your way back home after taking a trailer load of alcohols.
Now hand me the phone this very minute!"

So this is it! This is the point where I have to be killed for no cause.

Why don't they understand that I really want to return back the phone but my hand wouldn't just let me.

Just when the man raised his long gun to hit me, the young lady stopped him.

"Sir wait!"

The man paused and slowly brought his hand down. "Is anything wrong? Don't worry he will definitely return back the phone after I am done teaching him a lesson"

"Uh-mm.. I..it is okay sir, I know how to handle this" She stuttered.

"What? Do you think I am a joke? I came here wasting my time to help such a cunt like you?"

" I am sorry sir"

" You think he is ever gonna bring it out? Ohhh no! damn it. I am out of here.
Fuck off bitch!"

Thank God he is leaving. Such a psycho. I let out a sigh of relief as I watched him go back into the forest and disappeared into thin air. I wonder if he is not scared of the wild life that dwells in such forest.

My eyes fell on the young lady standing before me. There was something strange about her. Are all humans this kind? No, I don't think so. Not after meeting that miserable security guard.

"Hey it's okay. I know you can't be able to move your hands: maybe because you drank yourself to stupor or maybe you're sick or something. But it is okay. Can I just take the phone myself?"

Why is she so nice? I nodded my head as a sign of being positive to the question she asked. She moved closer to where I stood and I couldn't help but inhale the amazing fragrance of her cologne.

She put her hand into the pocket and took it out gently, then she smiled at me and for a moment and without thinking twice, I lifted up my hand to touch her soft plump cheek.

"You can move your hands? " She exclaimed excitedly, making me pause.

What is wrong with me? I quickly brought down my hand.

"You don't have to be shy" She giggled. "I'm Sophia, What is your name?"

A name? Oh, that is right. I don't even have a name. And even if I have one, I just can't remember any.

"You can't talk?. Oh. You're tired and can't talk now. It is okay, probably when next we meet. I will be leaving now. Do take care of yourself with the little cash in the hoodie OK?"

I nodded again. She smiled broadly at me, revealing her neatly arranged white teeth before she finally turned and walked away.
I couldn't stop smiling at her the moment she left, even though she turns her back occasionally to smile back. Just then, I was distracted by the noise and aroma of people around. It seems there is a movie about to be shown in the cinema and everyone was busy moving in and out of the big hall.
I let out a deep breath and looked into the cinema, a few meters away from where I stood. I saw the magnificent projector they use in displaying movie. It was so mighty.

I was still admiring the magnificent projector and suddenly, the movie showing in it caught my attention! It was actually a vampire movie.

I saw how vampires were being killed ruthlessly without mercy. I paused a bit in horror while imagining the cruelty of humans. Is this how I am going to end?! Is it?! Oh no. I can't continue being this way I must train myself to be strong enough and have a control over my body and urges. I should find a cure to my miserable life! I cant let this savage humans get a hold of my life.

I turned around and I saw a house just a stone throw from where i stood. I didn't even notice it all these while.

I quickly scurried over to the house. I saw fire at the middle of the compound, maybe the inhabitants are cooking I guess, but there is no one there just a pot on a fire.

I saw where they hanged their clothes outside and I took all of them, they should have additional clothes inside. I also managed to carry the heavy firewood I saw; it was too heavy, but I had to roll it fast enough back to the rainforest.

I just hope I don't get caught again by the psycho who calls himself forest guard.

I rolled it in a direction i felt the forest guard may not be. suddenly, I lost control of my body, the hunger sensation took over me. The sensation in me craved for blood.

 I lost control and I wasn't able to do anything. I saw a rabbit on a tree and then, few seconds later, my brain went blank.

CHAPTER THREE

introduction

I felt a very bright sensation trying to pierce through my eyes and I covered my eyes with the back of my hands and opened one of the eyes a bit tiny and the other completely closed. Oh! its morning already.

 I turned around and I saw the head of a dead rabbit, it's blood was already dried and it's body was gone. I slowly looked down at my hands and was shocked to see blood stains on them.

 Oh no! I ate this stuff?
How could I ? I even ate it raw, maybe I even ate it alive. I felt so disgusted as I tried to remember what really happened.

I couldn't recall anything but I believe that I am the one that eat this gibberish on the ground. Although I remembered seeing a rabbit last night, but my brain went blank after that.

What the heck is happening to me? I have to do something before I lose my sanity.

I started working on myself immediately. I brought little sticks and forced them into my mouth; to enable my mouth open freely at will. I used the heavy wood I rolled into the rainforest as dumbbell.

As I was about lifting the wood the second time, I lost balance and I fell down. So tiring.

A glass mirror fell out of the pocket of the hoodie, and I picked it up carefully, only to look into it and find out that my face looked exactly like that of the humans.

This means that nobody would suspect me unless they catch me feeding on flesh right?

Gosh! How can I control my urges?.

Just then, my mind went to the incident that happened yesterday. When that lady came closer to me to take her phone, I didn't have any urges. Although, I perceived a great aroma from her but there was no urges. I was even able to move my hands.

Could this be that?..

****

SOPHIA'S POV

Sorry for the late introduction; I am Sophia Chidora popularly called Sophia by my small circle. I am twenty two years old and I am happy with my life.

I live with my nagging elder sister Gwen Chidora in her matrimonial home. she has two kids a boy and a girl; just the type I would love to have in the nearest future. Her husband Felix was unemployed but seems the situation is more complicated than I can say; you will get to know with time.

I worked as a journalist in Frankfurt, a job that is unsatisfying to Gwen my sister. she would always walk into my room with her brown blond hair and slim shaped figure, just to remind me that she didn't sacrifice everything for me to go to school and become a journalist.

"Gwen-eve, I always wanted to be a journalist it's not like I ended up unfortunately into the field. I promise to make you proud one day"

I always said that with a smile that showed my perfectly arranged white teeth that everyone always commended on.

"just have a little faith sister, it's going to be OK"

I myself wasn't sure of what the future had for me, but I know it's not something good.

Gwen always replied my kind words with hot Savage replies, but who cares; I have lived with it all my life. I only cover my ears with my soft fur pillows whenever she yells at me.

I think she enjoys the yelling or should I say it's a part of her. Her children and husband equally covers their ear whenever she starts to yell. In fact, her husband bought an ear muff to help him adjust her pitch whenever she yells.

Nevertheless, Gwen is a loving sister, mother and wife, just that she took after my mother's temperament. our parents died in a car accident when she was nine, and then, I was just four years old. she sacrificed her own education just to make sure I survived in Bayern munichen.

to crown it all, she is the back bone behind my education.

she had a small mall in front of the house where she sell candies, and ice cream to children. she also sews clothe for people.

"Sophia! Sophiaaaaaa! Sophia!"

her voice was now my morning alarm everyday. it always rings in my head every morning, piercing through my ear drums.

I can't just get used to it, it's unbearable.

I stepped into my purple designed slippers and I walked directly towards the mirror.

I untied my black hair and allowed it to scatter all over my neck like the wilderness. I observed my curves by using my hands to go on it slowly.

I left for the dining room immediately I heard my name one more time to avoid her morning yelling. but it's of no use; she will still yell for yelling sake.

It was already 8:10 am and I was a bit late for work!
I waved down a nearby taxi in a haste. but before I could enter, I heard a familiar voice yelling my name and coming after me.

ohhhhh not again, what have I done to Gwen this time around. "you fool! you left your phone on the birth room, what were you thinking Hugh!? I wonder how your boss manages you.

before she could finish pouring out the rain in her mouth which will never stop, I hugged her and shouted thank 'danke' (thank you in German).

then I entered the taxi and the driver saved me the rest of the hot savages.

My boss, Mr. Franklin was already in my office going through my little library, the moment I opened the door. He gave out a horrific smile a sign that he recognized my presence.

I always expected him to be there in my office whenever I am a minute late, but I didn't just expect him that day.

"miss chidora this is the fifty seventh time"

he is the only one that calls me by that name. He has a funny habit of coming to my office whenever I haven't arrived early; and this is the 57th time he is doing it. He was expecting an explanation as usual so I tried to give him the best possible and justifiable reason, then he cut me off sharply and rudely

"Keep your explanations to yourself young woman I don't think I want to hear it" he horled looking directly into my eyes with his mean red eyes. My face went stale and the words in my mouth all tumbled back to my stomach.

Suddenly he started smiling, just like a person possessed with demons, he started laughing; I should be horrified, but that was not the first time he was acting weird.

"fifty seventh time...!" he whispered to my ears and then left my office.

Mr. Franklin was the head of the Agency. He was about seven feet tall and he was light skinned with an amazing dark glittering hair that he always shows off. he was actually a mean man nonetheless.

My boyfriend, Felix also worked in the same place with me. but he stays in the down floor. he is the smartest worker and Mr. Franklin respects him more than anyone in the agency.

"gbam"
the door of my office opened with a little force.
it was Mr. Franklin again; why Is he always acting as almighty!?
"miss chidora, we have a work shift to you.

this is a murder case of a little girl that was murdered during the Christmas period last year. I am giving you this case to handle"

I went mute for about three seconds, then he raised his eyebrows

"OK sir... I ... I...I will try my best sir"
he turned around to leave the office, but it was as if he remembered something.

"miss chidora"

"yes....yess sir"

"we don't try our best in this agency. we do our best."

"yes Mr Franklin....oohhh sorry yes sir"

I have grown the uncanny attitude of addressing him as Mr Franklin even though he has instructed me not to do so again, it just keeps coming to my mind.

I took a deep breath, then I tried to get the file Mr. Franklin dropped on my table..
then again my office door goes open with another force.

this time it was My boyfriend trying to act like Mr Franklin.
he gave out a gentle and loud laughter when he saw how scary I was.
"you fool! you want to give me a high blood pressure!?"

"yes I do! scary cat" he said while still laughing.
he made himself comfortable in my office and sat down with legs crossed on my table.

"seems you got a new contract from the boss.
can you handle it alone?"

"I was actually going to come around and ask you to assist me, but that's if you don't come up with your silly conditions."

Felix has a silly attitude of always asking me to make him hot coffee every morning, whenever I seek for his assistant.

"he gave out a louder smile this time around, but why!?
is it too hard to ask for?"
he was still laughing out loud when Mr Franklin entered the office with a straight face.

"hey you two love birds, this is no free hour, get to work this very minute"
"yes... yesssss....sieeer" Felix said with a shivering voice.

I laughed uncontrollably the moment Mr Franklin passed the office.

"now who is the scary cat..?" I was still laughing uncontrollably when he left the office.
he banged the door behind him and shouted from outside "I am not going to assist you Sophia"
 "yes you will fool!" I shouted back at him in great amusement.

I was so happy and I don't know why.

when it was noon, I decided to look into the investigation that Mr. Franklin gave me

well I didn't know how to go about the job, but i know something must be done about it.

first, I decided to settle out issues with my boyfriend.

When it was noon, I decided to pay him a surprise visit.

I sneaked to the last floor from the second floor where my office was allocated.

lo and behold, I saw him talking with Gwen.

"Gwen!?.." I muttered in surprise.

I know she usually comes around in the office to bring my lunch and then gift free ice creams to my co-workers but she came a bit earlier today and I wasn't hungry.

There is no way I had a choice whenever Gwen brings me lunch... it's either I finish it up calmly in her presence or she forces me to do it after shouting half of the office down.

"There she is!..." she shouted as she saw me.

"sis you know you don't have to keep doing this everyday; I am no longer a baby I am twenty two for crying out loud!"

I noticed she was cooking some hot words in her mouth then I decided to bail my self from eating the lunch she brought..

"and then guess what sis?..." I smiled at her

"what..." she let out the word while still gazing at me with great hunger to start lashing me with her Savage words.

"I already had lunch with Felix... so my stomach is full now" I turned my gaze to Felix, begging him with my eyeballs not to let my guards down.

Felix let out a funny laughter and I thought he was going to blow it...

"ohhh yeah... Gwen we already had lunch" he said scratching his head.

"ohhhhh what a nice in-law when will you come and marry this good for nothing girl!?"

"but we still need your sweet and delicious ice cream sis!"

I had to cheap in to prevent her marriage lectures

"now you call it delicious after abandoning your portion today during breakfast"
 she tried to draw my hair's as she said it but I was at Alert; I know my sister more than she knows herself; I took to my heels and we ran round Felix office till everywhere and everyone was stained with ice cream and we were all sitting on the couch laughing except for Felix who was enjoying the ice cream licking his hands while sitting on the ground. He seems to be more excited than the both of us.

CHAPTER FOUR

Back To The Woods

MICHAEL'S POV

I spent the last two years in the forest, learning how to behave like the humans and doing things the human way, but I still got one problem; I can't eat cooked food I only eat raw meals...

all the while I was in the forest,I couldn't take my mind off the last human being I saw; the girl that I took her hoodie. I still kept the hoodie with me though.

lost in deep thoughts, I heard an unusual sound coming from the south region of the forest. At first,I thought it was the forest guard but on a second thought, the forest guard had retired a year ago and no replacement that I know is available for his position.

I decided to go have a look... probably it may be a good meal for me.

I tip toed to the area and I saw a man on black cloak, kneeling and paying homage to a grave... well thank God I have had my dinner; I was able to overcome the aroma from his body.

As I was about leaving, another man on a longer black cloak arrived the scene from nowhere and attacked the man who was kneeling.

He killed the man who was kneeling after he had hit the man's head so many times on a rock, he spat on him and left the scene into nowhere, just as he arrived. I was astonished!

Here I am trying so hard to be like humans, and there are humans trying so hard to be like vampires to themselves.

I moved closer to the man who was almost dead. He was trying to say things to me but I couldn't understand the sounds he was making. I tried to understand, but he died in my arms the moment I tried.

I searched the man's cloak pocket and I found a key with an ID.
"Mr Romeo Ken the manager of Romeo's Detective Agency"
just as I read the details in the ID, an idea hit me.

I decided that I was going to become the next Mr Romeo. I will replace him since he was dead anyways; on a second thought, why was he killed? could I also be killed for the same reason which he was being killed ? a reason I don't even know? Well maybe it could help me in my journey of self discovery.

Dressed in Mr Romeo's Detective wear, I left the forest and was heading to the location of the agency which was clearly written in the ID. I wore his hat to cover my face In-case anybody notices anything wired about me... anyways it's night who would?

I got to the Agency after walking so many miles, the interesting thing is that I wasn't tired. But I shouldn't be surprised, I don't think I am same with humans.

It wasn't a fancy place as I thought, but it's a place I can rest my head for a while before I can discover who I am.

I saw his Billboard and I went straight to the door right below it. I slide the key inside the lock to open it, "Mr Romeo?" I shivered at the sound of the name, knowing fully well that the person was referring to me. I had to do something before I raise any suspense.

"oi I am not in the mood to talk now... let's talk later" I quickly replied, hoping that it will work although I know it won't.
"you scum bag! you told me to wait right here for you only for you to come back here and bullshit me?"
I had to play along "oi that's right, Mr man, I will just go inside

and get a few things and then I will come out for us to talk OK?"

"don't bullshit me Mr Romeo! you now call me Mr man as well?"

he gave out a dangerous gasp before he continued

"look Mr Romeo, if you go into that house and you don't bring your rent fee while coming out, then I should expect that you already want me to force you out of my building!"

ahhhhh this is the real owner of the house? so Mr Romeo was a tenant anyway, I thought he was so rich, just as he was dressed. Now I have gotten into a whole lot of problem which I don't know how to start handling it.

I was hit with a thought to feed on the mans blood… I had to fight the urge with every energy I have got in me

"NO!" I spoke out without thinking.

The man right before me thought I was referring to him, "No?

No to what exactly Mr Romeo. I have had enough patience with you and I think I have run out of patience.

Look, enter that goddamn office of yours and get me my money or get ready to get your filthy self kicked out of my building! OK?"

I was puzzled. I didn't know what I should do or say to the mean looking man. Maybe I should just leave him to take back his property and go back to the woods where I have been. On a second thought, I can beg him for some time; probably, I can find a way to source out the money I will give to him. Well it all depends if he agrees to spare me the time.

"sorry Mr? How much am I owing you again Mr?"

I wanted to know if the money was what I can source out by impersonating the broke Mr Romeo. Did I just say broke? Well, I don't know, but I think he is broke, if not, he should have soughted out his rent.

"look Mr Romeo, I will only give you the grace of tonight only because of the respect that i have for you. But one more drunk questions about how much you owe, i will send you parking tonight!"

"huhg" I gasped as the man left.

I opened the door to the office and it was neatly arranged and well scented. It had a very cool library that was well fashioned.

I sat on his chair and opened his laptop

THIS STORY WILL BE UPDATED SOON THANK YOU